D0824746

SPORTS SCIENCE

Soccer Science

Natalie Hyde

Crabtree Publishing Company

www.crabtreebooks.com

Crabtree Publishing Company

www.crabtreebooks.com

Author: Natalie Hyde

Editors: Molly Aloian
Leon Gray

Proofreaders: Adrianna Morganelli
Robert Walker

Project coordinator: Robert Walker

Production coordinator: Margaret Amy Salter

Prepress technician: Margaret Amy Salter

Designer: Lynne Lennon

Picture researcher: Sean Hannaway

Managing editor: Tim Cooke

Art director: Jeni Child

Design manager: David Poole

Editorial director: Lindsey Lowe

Children's publisher: Anne O'Daly

Photographs:
Action Images: David Gray: page 7 (left); Marcos Brindicci: page 7 (right); Paul Harding: pages 8, 13 (top), 23 (bottom); Eric Bretagnon: page 13 (bottom); Victor Fraile: page 15 (bottom); Jean-Paul Pelissier: pages 20–21; Petr Josek: pages 24-25; Wolfgang Rattay: page 26; Ronen Zvulun: page 28
Corbis: Dann Tardif: page 21
Getty Images: Bob Thomas: pages 5 (top), 27 (top); Bob Levey: page 5 (bottom); Laurence Griffiths: pages 6–7; Mark Scott: pages 8–9; Hrvoje Polan: page 10; Christof Koepsel: page 11 (top); Stephen Dunn: page 12; Michael Kappeler: pages 16–17; Cancan Chu: page 18; Stu Forster: page 22; Thomas Lohnes: page 25; Bongarts: page 27 (bottom); AFP: page 29 (top)
PA Photos: Mike Egerton: page 14; Michael Steele: page 19 (top); Owen Humphreys: page 19 (bottom); PA Archive: page 24; Joerg Sarbach: page 29 (bottom)
Science Photo Library: GustoImages: page 11 (bottom)
Shutterstock: Yurlov Andrey Aleksandrovich: front cover; Albo: backgrounds, page 4; Tatjana Brila: page 15 (top)
Victor Maccharoli: page 23 (top)

Illustrations:
Mark Walker: page 17

Every effort has been made to trace the owners of copyrighted material.

Library and Archives Canada Cataloguing in Publication

Hyde, Natalie, 1963-
   Soccer science / Natalie Hyde.

(Sports science)
Includes index.
ISBN 978-0-7787-4537-2 (bound).--ISBN 978-0-7787-4554-9 (pbk.)

   1. Soccer--Juvenile literature. 2. Sports sciences--Juvenile literature.
I. Title. II. Series: Sports science (St. Catharines, Ont.)

GV943.25.H93 2008   j796.33401'5   C2008-907024-0

Library of Congress Cataloging-in-Publication Data

Hyde, Natalie, 1963-
   Soccer science / Natalie Hyde.
      p. cm. -- (Sports science)
   Includes index.
   ISBN 978-0-7787-4554-9 (pbk. : alk. paper) -- ISBN 978-0-7787-4537-2 (reinforced library binding : alk. paper)
   1. Soccer--Juvenile literature. 2. Sports sciences--Juvenile literature.
I. Title. II. Series.

GV943.25.H94 2008
796.334--dc22

                          2008046276

Crabtree Publishing Company
www.crabtreebooks.com   1-800-387-7650

Published in Canada
Crabtree Publishing
616 Welland Ave.
St. Catharines, Ontario
L2M 5V6

Published in the United States
Crabtree Publishing
PMB16A
350 Fifth Ave., Suite 3308
New York, NY 10118

Contents

Introducing Soccer

What started out as a game for off-duty soldiers has become the most popular sport on the planet. People play soccer in almost every country in the world. Today, more than three billion people enjoy the game.

The modern sport of soccer began in England in 1863. Since then, the rules have essentially stayed the same, but the game is faster and the players are more skilled and in much better shape.

Fans enjoy a game at the Meazza Stadium in Milan, Italy.

LOOK CLOSER

Mob football

Mob football was an early form of soccer played by an unlimited number of people from neighboring villages. The idea of the game was for players from one village to move the ball to the other village's square. Mob football was violent, with few rules and many injuries. Riots were so common that many kings tried to ban the game.

Soccer science

Science plays an important role in the sport. Fitness experts have improved training techniques so players can perform at their best.

Soccer gear

Soccer gear has improved. **Synthetic** materials are used to make lighter, stronger shoes, shin guards and jerseys that help to keep the players cool. Even the ball has changed. Players have more control with the new tough, long-lasting balls. This has made the game more enjoyable for both fans and players.

➡ *Soccer players need to be fit to keep up with the game.*

NEW WORDS

Synthetic: Something that is produced by people and not found in nature.

Soccer Fitness

Professional soccer players must be fit to play the full 90 minutes. Soccer is a game of constant movement, so players need a balance of power and strength to succeed. Strong muscles will give them the stamina to last through the game. Explosive power will allow them to sprint, turn, kick, and jump quickly.

The main way to improve stamina is through **aerobic exercise**. Muscles need oxygen to work. The harder they work, the more oxygen they use. Aerobic exercises make the heart strong. A strong heart can bring oxygen-rich blood to tired muscles faster.

Ronaldinho sprints to meet a long pass.

NEW WORDS

Aerobic exercise: A type of exercise that improves the way in which the body uses oxygen.

Plyometrics

Soccer players need power for quick turns and sprints. A muscle that has stretched before it tightens moves more powerfully. This is what **plyometric exercises** do. They help muscles to stretch and tighten strongly and quickly.

Jump!

Try this plyometric exercise. Bend your knees slowly and then try to jump as high as you can. Try it again, only this time bend your knees quickly and jump. Can you notice the difference? Quick stretching and tightening gives you more power to jump higher.

LOOK CLOSER

Depth jumps

One plyometric exercise is called the "depth jump." Players jump from a platform about six feet (two meters) above the ground and try to spring back up again as soon as they hit the ground.

Plyometric exercises improve strength and power.

FACT!

Heart facts

At rest, a player might have a heart rate as low as 40 beats per minute. Sprinting at full speed, the rate might rise to 180 beats per minute. This reflects the amount of work the heart must do to meet the increased demands of the body during the game.

Plyometric exercise: A type of exercise training designed to produce fast, powerful movements.

Soccer Skills

Soccer players need more than speed and stamina. They need balance, fast reaction times, and excellent skills, such as ball control.

Dribbling is a vital soccer skill. Players use small kicks to move the ball down the pitch while they are running. Players can teach their muscles to move in a certain way to control the ball while sprinting. Coaches use drills to help the players develop these skills. By practicing a movement over and over, the body will react faster during the game. Players also need to see everything around them when they are dribbling. They use their **peripheral vision** to kick the ball without looking down.

Soccer drills help players develop good ball control.

An acrobatic overhead kick requires balance and coordination.

▶ ▶ ▶ ▶ ▶ ▶ ▶ ▶

Record breaker

Martinho Orige of Brazil holds the Guinness World record for juggling a soccer ball. In 2003, Orige juggled a ball nonstop for 19 hours and 30 minutes with his feet, legs, and head.

Balance and coordination

Soccer players must move quickly without falling, so they need good balance. Some players use a wobble board to help them learn to stay balanced. The brain uses many different body parts to maintain balance. The ears, eyes, joints, skin, and muscles all send information to the brain. The brain then decides which parts should move. All this happens in a fraction of a second. Good coordination is also important. All the different parts of the player's body work together quickly and smoothly. Coordination between the feet and eyes is controlled by the brain. Information from the eyes travels quickly on pathways in the brain. These pathways are forged on the soccer pitch (field). This is how a soccer player is able to perform skills so easily.

LOOK CLOSER

Ball juggling

Soccer ball juggling is a good way to practice ball control. By trying to keep the ball off the ground, players learn how hard or soft they need to hit it. They also learn to use different parts of their bodies to move the ball.

NEW WORDS

Peripheral vision: The ability to see at the margins of the normal field of vision.

9

Soccer Fuel

The body is a machine that needs fuel to perform. Food gives us energy for our brains, muscles, and other organs. Soccer players who eat the right foods will perform better than players who do not.

The best foods for sports give the body a steady supply of energy. **Carbohydrates** are the main source of energy for our bodies. They help regulate our blood sugar levels. This helps keep muscles from getting tired. Potatoes and oatmeal are high in carbohydrates.

Croatian players take a lunch break after an intensive training session.

FACT! Fluid facts

Soccer players lose up to seven pints (four liters) of fluid during a match. This is why it is so important to keep drinking.

Drinking plenty of fluids is essential to prevent dehydration.

Storing glucose

The body burns energy from food in the form of a sugar called glucose. Any glucose that is not needed is stored inside the body as glycogen. When the body runs out of glucose, it uses the stored glycogen.

Keep drinking

Soccer players lose a lot of body fluids during a game through sweat. Most body organs cannot work without enough fluid. Dehydration is a danger for athletes. Fluids need to be replaced quickly so that sore joints and muscles can be repaired. Even a little dehydration will affect a soccer player's game.

Isotonic drinks are the best way for players to replace lost fluids. These drinks are even better than water. They have carbohydrates and a little salt for energy. Scientific studies have shown that these drinks help muscles heal quicker than drinking water alone.

All these foods are rich in carbohydrates.

LOOK CLOSER

Soccer supplements

Some soccer players use supplements. Some of these pills and powders help the body heal faster. Others help to build muscle. Some have serious side effects. The best way to get everything the body needs is to eat a healthy diet.

NEW WORDS

Carbohydrates: Substances in food made from carbon, hydrogen, and oxygen.

11

Will to Win

Los Angeles Galaxy striker Landon Donovan prepares for a penalty kick to win the match.

Today's soccer players are under a lot of pressure to win. There is a lot at stake when they play. A good season means championships, more money, and pride. There are also deep club rivalries. Players want to win for their team or country. No amount of individual skill matters if a player cracks under pressure and misses an important shot.

Soccer players must train their minds as well as their bodies if they are going to succeed. Great ball control and good balance will not help a player who is afraid to fail. Most of the professional clubs hire a **sport psychologist**. He or she talks to the players about how they think before, during, and after the match.

Brain scans show that people use different parts of their brain for different things. One part is used for learning new movements — another for skills that have already been learned. It takes time for the brain to switch between them. If a player has not practiced the skill, he or she may miss an important shot.

NEW WORDS ● ● ● ● ● ● ● ● ● ● ● ● ● ● ● ● ●

Sport psychologist: A doctor who is trained to improve the mental attitude of athletes.

➡️ *Players gather in a huddle for a team talk to get ready for an important game.*

Visualization

Many players train their minds using a process called visualization. In their minds, they picture themselves scoring the match-winning goal. Imagining it is almost the same as scoring in real life. The same pathways in the brain are created. When the time comes to score the goal in a match, the mind is ready.

⬇️ *Players win important games by believing in their abilities.*

LOOK CLOSER

Nervous start

It is perfectly normal to be nervous before an important game. Some players use deep breathing to stay calm and focused. This helps to increase blood flow to the brain and other organs.

FACT!

▶ ▶ ▶ ▶ ▶ ▶ ▶ ▶

Superstitions

Many soccer players are **superstitious**. Many have lucky shoes or socks that they always wear for matches. One player might jump over all the white lines on the pitch before the start of the game. Another might wear his or her underwear inside out to ensure good luck!

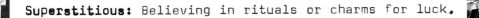

Superstitious: Believing in rituals or charms for luck.

13

Soccer Bag

Soccer gear has come a long way since the earliest players from Victorian times wore top hats and baggy shorts. Scientists have invented new materials and better ways of making the players' equipment. Modern gear is lighter, cooler, and more durable.

Shin guards are long enough to protect the leg from the knee to the ankle. They are made of **polyurethane**. Padding inside is raised a little to help keep the leg cool.

Better jerseys

Early jerseys were made from cotton. Cotton would hold in sweat, making the jerseys uncomfortable. Modern jerseys are made of **synthetic fibers**. The fibers form a mesh that keeps sweat away from the body and lets cool air circulate.

Soccer star David Beckham pulls his socks over his shin guards before taking a kick.

NEW WORDS

Polyurethane: A hard plastic that can be molded into different shapes.

Soccer shoes are the most important part of the players' equipment

Soccer shoes

A soccer player's feet do most of the work, so the shoes must be tough. Early shoes were made of leather, with long laces and a hard toecap. Metal studs helped them grip muddy ground. Modern shoes are made of synthetic materials or kangaroo leather. The inside of the shoe has a cushion in the middle. The cushion consists of fluids and gas inside a special material. The outside of the soccer shoe has changed, too. Modern shoes are shorter and softer so the foot can move better. Eyelets and laces are flatter so there is more control when a ball hits the top of the foot.

The players' number and team logo adorn the jersey.

FACT!

Against the rules

Players are not allowed to wear jewelry or watches. These items might cause injuries to themselves or other players.

LOOK CLOSER

Goalie gear

The goalie's shorts have more padding and are longer than the shorts of other players. This helps to protect the goalie from bruises and cuts. Padded gloves prevent injury and help grip the ball.

Synthetic fibers: Human-made textiles such as nylon.

All About the Ball

Early balls were made of animal bladders filled with air. The balls were tough, but the shape was not perfect. This made the ball move in unpredictable ways. Soccer balls have come a long way since then.

The core of a soccer ball is still called a bladder. Today, bladders are made of latex or butyl instead of animal body parts. Latex is softer than butyl, but it does not hold air as well. So it has to be blown up more often. The **valve** is important, too. A good valve will not leak out all the air. The best ones are butyl covered with **silicone**.

The lining surrounds the bladder. There are several layers of lining in a ball. The better the ball, the more layers of lining it has. This is what gives the ball its strength and bounce.

LOOK CLOSER

Match ball
Each match at the 2006 World Cup finals had its own unique ball. Each one had the date, the stadium, and the team names printed on it. The final featured a special gold-colored ball.

This gold ball was used in the final of the 2006 World Cup.

NEW WORDS

Silicone: A strong, flexible, water-resistant plastic.

Cover up

Modern covers are synthetic leather. This keeps the ball light — even in wet weather. Old leather covers used to soak up water, making the ball heavier.

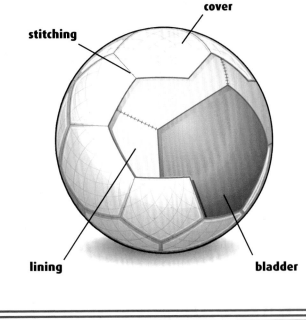

stitching · cover · lining · bladder

⬆ *The four main parts of a soccer ball are the bladder, the lining, the cover, and the stitching.*

Ball panels

Different balls have different numbers of panels. They are stitched, glued, or molded together. The panels bulge and give the ball its round shape when it is filled with air.

Ball regulations

Regulation balls have a stamp that says "FIFA approved" or "official size and weight." These balls have been tested in a laboratory to make sure they are made correctly.

Valve: An opening through which air can be blown to inflate a ball.

Kicking the Ball

▲ **A ball bends around a wall of defenders.**

Kicking the ball is one of the most basic soccer skills. But players do much more than just punt the ball down the pitch. They can make the ball go in any direction — fast or slow. They do this by changing what part of the foot they use to kick the ball and how much force they put behind the kick.

It is better to strike the ball with the side of the foot than with the toe. The toe presents only a small area of the foot, so there is less control over the ball. The side of the foot has more surface area hitting the ball. Hitting the ball on the sides also creates spin.

▶ ▶ ▶ ▶ ▶ ▶ ▶ ▶

FACT!

Soccer rocks

The *Apollo 17* astronauts played soccer on the moon. They used a 200-pound (90-kilogram) rock as a soccer ball. On Earth, they would have broken their feet. There is less gravity on the moon, so the rock seemed lighter.

NEW WORDS

Air pressure: The force created by the weight of air pushing against an object.

Curving kicks

In a banana kick, the ball is made to bend around a wall of defenders and into the back of the net. It is as if there is a magnet pulling the ball.

Bending the ball is not magic. It is physics. When a ball spins, one side of it spins in the same direction as the air around it. This side has less **air pressure**. Since the ball will always move toward low pressure, it curves slightly. The slower a ball moves through the air, the more its path will curve. This bending is called the Magnus effect.

Slowing down

A ball moves fast at the beginning of a kick and then slows down. So the bending might be slight to begin with, but the ball bends more as it slows down. This is why a banana kick seems to bend so suddenly.

Roberto Carlos uses the Magnus effect to kick a curving free kick.

A lot of skill is required to kick a ball on the volley.

LOOK CLOSER

Penalty put-offs

Goalies will do things to distract players waiting to take penalty kicks. A player has to concentrate even if the goalie is jumping up and down. The most important thing to do is to stay calm. Studies have shown that the best place to aim the kick is high into the corner of the net. Even if the goalie knows it's coming, he or she will not have time to stop it.

Magnus effect: The curved path of a moving object caused by its own rotation.

Heading the Ball

Heading the ball is a skill unique to soccer. During a soccer game, the ball is in the air a lot of the time. Controlling the ball in the air is important. In professional games, many of the goals come from headers.

The best way to head the ball is to use the forehead. Just like the side of the foot is better than the toe for kicking because more area touches the ball, the forehead is larger and flatter than other parts of the head. It is also the thickest part of the skull and the safest for absorbing the **impact**. Neck muscles should be tight and still so the head does not snap back when the ball hits. This also helps the head absorb the **kinetic energy** of the moving ball. A player makes the ball fly off in a new direction by giving it new kinetic energy. If a player is standing still and heads the ball, it will not go far. A player should jump up to meet the ball and thrust forward with the body. The ball will then go much farther.

NEW WORDS ● ● ● ● ● ● ● ● ● ● ● ● ● ● ● ●

Impact: The force resulting from the collision of two or more objects.

LOOK CLOSER

Soft skull

Most coaches recommend that children do not head the ball. The skull of a young person is not as hard as the skull of an adult. The main concern is crashing heads with another player when they both try to head the same ball. The brain may also "slush" up against the skull when the player heads the ball.

Two players jump up to meet the ball.

Attack and defense

For an attacking header, a player needs to keep the head downward to angle the ball into the back of the net. In a defensive header, a player wants the ball to go high and away from the goal. So the head needs to be slightly under the ball when the player makes contact.

FACT!

▶ ▶ ▶ ▶ ▶ ▶ ▶

Record breaker

The Guinness World Record for heading a ball without it dropping is eight hours, 32 minutes, and three seconds. It is held by Tomas Lundman of Sweden.

Kinetic energy: The energy an object has because it is moving.

Throwing In

Usually only the goalie can touch the ball with the hands. But there are two times in a soccer game when other players can do the same. One is to set a ball for a free kick. The other is for a throw-in.

Alvaro Arbeloa takes a throw-in for Liverpool during a UEFA Champions League match.

There are two kinds of throw-ins: the running throw-in and the standing throw-in. Both feet must be touching the ground when the player releases the ball. If one foot is off the ground, the referee will call a foul throw. The ball is then given to the other team.

LOOK CLOSER

Flip throw-ins

Players use the entire body as a lever to make a flip throw-in (see right). Some people believe more power can be achieved this way. However, the extra **velocity** means there is less control over where the ball ends up. There is also a bigger chance the throw-in will be illegal. Often both feet are not on the ground or the thrower is sitting on the ground. Although flip throw-ins are not against the rules, many soccer leagues do not allow them.

➡ *The ball is thrown from behind and over the head with both hands*

Propelling the ball

The idea of a throw-in is to get the most velocity and accuracy. Velocity is determined by how hard the ball is thrown. The power behind the throw is found in the muscles and joints of the player. The arms, shoulders, and hips all help the player create more velocity.

Run for it

Most of the time younger players get better results from running throw-ins. Professional players have stronger muscles in their arms and shoulders. They can get as much or more speed from a standing throw-in.

NEW WORDS

Velocity: A measure of the speed and direction of a moving object.

Keeping Goal

Keeping the ball out of the goal is just as important as scoring goals. The goalie is the last line of defense. The goalie requires skills that are completely different from the other players on the pitch.

Footwork is the key to good goalkeeping. If a goalie cannot get to the ball, he or she cannot stop it. For short distances, the shuffle step can be used to close the gap. The goalie steps sideways without crossing his or her feet.

LOOK CLOSER

Lev Yashin

Lev Yashin was voted the best goalkeeper of the 20th century. He helped the Soviet soccer team win gold at the 1956 Olympic Games and the 1960 European Championships. It is said he saved more than 150 penalty kicks during his career. Other players called him "Black Spider" because they saw him wearing all black and standing by the net.

NEW WORDS

Flexibility: The ability of a player to bend and stretch easily.

In this way, the goalie always faces the ball, with shoulders and hips pointing forward. When a goalie needs to move farther, he or she turns the hips and runs but keeps the shoulders facing toward the ball.

Stretching exercises help to improve flexibility.

▼ *Czech goalkeeper Martin Vaniak makes a spectacular diving save.*

Goalkeepers must be able to make split-second decisions. The ability to move suddenly or predict where the ball goes requires quick **reaction times**.

Staying flexible

A goalkeeper needs **flexibility** to make jumping and diving catches. There are two kinds of exercises to stretch muscles and improve flexibility. Ballistic stretches use bobbing movements that stretch the muscle farther each time. Static stretches hold the stretch for 15 to 30 seconds. Both types of stretches should be done every day. Sports scientists believe that the slow, gentle movements of static stretches are better for the body.

FACT!

What color?
Soccer goalies did not have to wear different-colored jerseys from their teammates until 1913.

Reaction time: The time it takes for the body to respond to something the eyes have seen.

The Perfect Pitch

Soccer is played on many surfaces, from sandy beaches to grass pitches. The surface makes a big difference to the game. It changes how quickly a player can run, stop, and turn. It also affects how the ball moves. The ball can roll faster or slower, bounce higher, or shoot off in any direction.

Workers lay new turf on a soccer pitch.

The perfect pitch would be a level grass field. The ground would be soft to allow the studs to dig in but firm for a good bounce. Many different things affect the quality of a grass pitch — weather, wear and tear, and even the **subsurface** layer beneath the grass.

Artificial grass

Real grass is hard to grow and expensive to keep. Some stadiums use artificial turf. Early artificial turf was hard and gave players **friction** burns when they fell. The ball did not bounce or roll the same way as on grass. Artificial turf is now much better. The ball behaves the same way, and players do not get injured.

NEW WORDS

Friction: The force that opposes movement over a surface.

The FIFA World Cup Stadium in Frankfurt, Germany, has a roof and video cube above the pitch.

Stadium safety

German scientists are studying crowded stadiums. They want to know how fast they can evacuate people if there is a problem. They watch the movements of fans using cameras. They hope to stop accidents where fans are crushed in crowds. In 1989, more than 90 fans died in this way at Hillsborough Stadium in England during a match between Liverpool and Nottingham Forest.

LOOK CLOSER

Mexican wave

The "Mexican wave" started out by accident at a National Hockey League game. Soccer fans first saw it at the Mexico World Cup in 1986. It takes about 25 people to start a wave by jumping to their feet with their hands in the air. The wave then races around the stadium at about 20 seats per second.

Subsurface: The layer just beneath the surface of the ground.

27

The Future of Soccer

S·cience is helping soccer become a faster, more precise, and more exciting sport. The future of the game looks bright for players and fans alike.

Coaches use the latest computer technology to study player performance.

Video playback helps soccer players study how they perform during a game. By looking at their mistakes they can make improvements. Players can also practice new skills using computer simulation.

Ticket sales are also changing. Future soccer events will use Radio Frequency IDentification tickets (RFIDs). These tickets can be scanned with a computer to make sure that they are not stolen or fake.

Helping the referee

Scientists are developing new systems to help referees make close calls. Hawk-Eye is a system of cameras pointed at the goal or foul lines. These cameras are better than the human eye at spotting the position of the ball. A German company has developed a new way to make close calls and not slow down the game. They have made a **microchip** that is implanted in the ball. There are sensors in the ground under the goal lines. These sensors can tell instantly when the ball has crossed the line. Then they can send the information to a unit worn by the referees. Some people believe technology will make the game fairer. Other people argue that using cameras and computers will slow down the game too much.

Soccer balls of the future may have microchips to help the referee make close calls.

LOOK CLOSER

RoboCup
RoboCup is an international soccer competition for robots. The robots can be very small or even human size. They are programmed to act on their own to decide strategies as they play games.

NEW WORDS

Microchip: A small crystal of silicon on which is etched tiny electronic circuits.

Glossary

aerobic exercise A type of exercise that improves the way in which the body uses oxygen

air pressure The force created by the weight of air pushing against an object

carbohydrates Substances in food made from carbon, hydrogen, and oxygen

flexibility The ability of a player to bend and stretch easily

friction The force that opposes movement over a surface

impact The force resulting from the collision of two or more objects

kinetic energy The energy an object has because it is moving

magnus effect The curved path of a moving object caused by its own rotation

microchip A small crystal of silicon on which is etched tiny electronic circuits

peripheral vision The ability to see at the margins of the normal field of vision

plyometric exercise A type of exercise training designed to produce fast, powerful movements

polyurethane A hard plastic that can be molded into different shapes

reaction time The time it takes for the body to respond to something the eyes have seen

silicone A strong, flexible, water-resistant plastic

sport psychologist A doctor who is trained to improve the mental attitude of athletes

subsurface The layer just beneath the surface of the ground

superstitious Believing in rituals or charms for luck

synthetic Something that is produced by people and not found in nature

synthetic fibers Human-made textiles such as nylon

valve An opening through which air can be blown to inflate a ball

velocity A measure of the speed and direction of a moving object

Find Out More

Books

Drewett, Jim. *How to Improve at Soccer.* New York: Crabtree Publishing Company, 2008.

Farrow, Pete, Eric Small, and Susan Saliba. *Soccer.* Broomall, Pennsylvania: Mason Crest Publishers, 2003.

Fridell, Ron. *Sports Technology (Cool Science).* Minneapolis, Minnesota: Lerner Publications, 2008.

Hornby, Hugh. *Soccer (DK Eyewitness Books).* New York: DK Children, 2008.

Thomas, Keltie. *How Soccer Works.* Toronto, Ontario: Maple Tree Press, 2007.

Wiese, Jim, and Ed Shems. *Sports Science: 40 Goal-Scoring, High-Flying, Medal-Winning Experiments for Kids.* New York: Wiley, 2002.

Web sites

The British Broadcasting Company's website explains the skills behind the sport of soccer, from passing and penalty kicks to tackling and turning.

http://news.bbc.co.uk/sport1/hi/football/skills/default.stm

This website includes a podcast that explains how to kick a bending kick, as well as a videoclip of Roberto Carlos and the *Apollo 17* astronauts playing soccer on the Moon.

http://www.sciencemadefun.org.uk/scienceofsoccer.html

Find out everything you need to know about soccer balls at SoccerBallWorld.com.

http://www.soccerballworld.com/

Index

Printed in the U.S.A. – BG